Diet recommendations for TCM - Stomach - Fire

Please check these recommendations always with a TCM nutrition consultant, therapist, doctor or dietician. The recipes and the list of ingredients are supporting also the conventional medical therapy. The calorie disclosures of fresh ingredients (fruit and vegetables) vary according to quality and time of harvest. The contents were checked by a dietician and a nutrition consultant for the Traditional Chinese Medicine (TCM).

Author:
©2017 Josef Miligui
www.ebns.at

AF285250

Source:
The lists are created from the EBNS database for nutritional counseling. The database is used by dietitians, therapists and doctors for advising the patient / client.

Literature:
The specialist literature and the training documents of the German and Austrian dietary and traditional Chinese medicine serve as a knowledge base. We have used the documents as a basis of knowledge, adapted it to our experience and completed them.
http://di-book.com

Title Photo:
©2008 Erika Weixlbaumer

Production and publishing:
BoD – Books on Demand, Norderstedt
ISBN: 9783752861457

Diet recommendations for TCM - Stomach - Fire

1   Treatment strategy

Cool stomach heat, channel stomach qi down and tonifies.
Hot NO, warm NO (except very little sweet spicy), all other YES

2   Avoid

Dairy products, pizza, ready meals, all spicy-bitter and salty hot / hot
spices, garlic, raw onions, salty and sour foods, alcohol, yogis, grilled,
fried, meat, toasted, coffee, chocolate, cocoa, cigarettes.

3   Breakfast

	kkal. per serving
Avocado with lemon	289
Baked chicory	230
Barley mash with plums	106
Black beans with avocado	263
Celery juice	33
Compote from apples	67
Cooling rice dish with grapefruit	234
Cous-Cous with date, coco and almondpuree	483
Cream cheese substitute	526
Cucumber soup	95
Italian champignon rice	256
Millet with egg and butter	338
Pear compote	100
Pear juice	180
Quick flakes with compote or jam	189
Radish with horseradish	196
Refreshing cucumber soup with potatoes	148
Reissue soup with duck	160
Rice congee with honey pear and black sesame	158
Rice congee with mung beans	424
Rice dulse soup	190
Rice porridge with orange peel	119

4   Snack

5   Lunch

6 Afternoon

7 Dinner

8 Any time

9 Recipes

(recommendable) = You can use more.
(little) = You should use less than specified or omit.

9.1   8 treasures of rice

Strengthens kidney and bladder, builds up Qi, strengthens the spleen, repels moisture, reduces internal heat, prevents cancer, builds heart, calms nerves.
Cooking time approx. 1 hour
Calories p. portion: 212
4 portions

Quantity of ingredients
Lily bulbs 1 table spoon / 5g. (recommended).................................. *
Longane 1 table spoon / 5g. (little)... *
King Solomon's-seal 1 table spoon / 5g. (recommended)................. *
Yam root, yam root tuber 1 table spoon / 5g. (recommended)........... *
Coix (seeds) YiYi Ren 1 table spoon / 5g. (yes)............................... *
Rice wild (nature rice) 1 1/2 cups / 240g. (yes) ....metal
Water 8-10 cups / 800g. (yes) .... earth

Cooking instructions:
Each one 1 tbsp: Bai He, Longan, Yu Zhu, Da Zao, Shan Yao, Lian Mi, Yi Yi Ren, Qian Shi
Add hot water and soak for about 30 minutes. Then add 1 - 2 cups of rice (normal) and simmer for 1/2 to 1 hour until the rice is very soft. Or: Cook for about 3 hours with the herbs a congee. Then the herbs do not have to be soaked.

9.2   Apple sauce with raisins

Nourishes fluids, reduces stomach heat, strengthens spleen, harmonizes stomach, moisturizes, relaxes, builds up Qi.
Cooking time approx. 25 min
Calories p. portion: 74
10 portions
Allergens: O

Quantity of ingredients
Apple (sweet) 2,2 lbs / 1000g. (yes)... earth
Water 1/2 cup / 100g. (yes) .... earth
Raisins 1/8 lbs - 2oz / 50g. (little)... earth

Cooking instructions:

Wash, peel and quarter the apples and remove the core. Put the apples with the water in a pot. Wash the raisins with hot water and add them. Cook at low heat for about 10 minutes, then allow to cool. For children up to 10 months, mash in the blender finely. For the larger ones, crush with the potato steamer. Fill and seal in a freezer or empty yoghurt jug. Close the yoghurt jug. Freeze in the shock freezer.

If necessary, thaw at room temperature for about 6 hours. (Lasting about 4 months).

The fruit mousse is intended as dessert or intermediate meal. It has an anti-digestive effect. In case of diarrhea give better banana.

9.3 Avocado with lemon

Nourishes Yin from liver, lung and colon, moisturizes, distributes, cools heat, preserves fluids, contracts.
Cooking time approx. 5 min
Calories p. portion: 289
1 portions

Quantity of ingredients

Avocado 1/2 piece / 120g. (recommended) .... earth
Lemon juice 1/2 piece / 10g. (yes) .... wood
Salt 1 pinch / 1g. (recommended) .... water

Cooking instructions:

Halve the avocado, remove the core, add the lemon juice, salt a little and eat with a spoon.

9.4 Baked chicory

Refreshing, brings the Qi down.
Cooking time approx. 20 min
Calories p. portion: 230
2 portions
Allergens: AG

Quantity of ingredients

Chicory 4 pieces / 500g. (recommended) .... fire
Cream, sweet 30% 2 table spoons / 40g. (little) .... *
Breadcrumbs (wheat bread) 2 table spoons / 20g. (yes) .... wood
Rice Basmati 1/2 cup / 60g. (yes) .... metal
Water 3 cups / 300g. (yes) .... earth
Salt 1 pinch / 1g. (recommended) .... water

Cooking instructions:
Blanch chicory in hot water whole for about 5 minutes; place in a casserole dish; put some sweet cream over it; put the bread crumbs over the chicory and gratinate.

Place the rice in salted water, heat till it boils and let it simmer over low heat for about 15 minutes.

9.5   Barley mash with plums

Forces spleen, cools bladder, diuretic, moisturizes intestines, relaxes, builds up Qi, spreads, strengthens blood and fluids, regulates Qi, cools liver fire, produces humors, strengthens Qi and Kidney Jing, moisturizes, relaxes, builds up Qi, spreads.
Cooking time approx. 25 min
Calories p. portion: 107
5 portions
Allergens: AG

Quantity of ingredients
Water 10 cups / 1200g. (yes).. earth
Barley 1 cup / 120g. (recommended)... earth
Plum 1 cup / 120g. (yes) ....wood
Butter organic 2 teaspoons / 6g. (yes) .... earth
Sugar cane sugar 1/2 teaspoon / 2g. (yes) .... earth

Cooking instructions:
Grind coarse the barley and roast it dry. Add hot water, add ginger and cardamom and let it swell to a pulp in low heat. Core the plums and boil for 10 minutes with a little water. At the end, add the stewed plums, a little butter and sweetener.

Variant: If you want to go fast, you can use barley flakes instead of shot.

9.6   Basic recipe for a beef broth (clear)

Strengthens Qi and Yang, is very warming.
Cooking time approx. 4-8 hours
Calories p. portion: 114
10 portions
Allergens: O

Quantity of ingredients

Beef soup meat 1,1 lbs / 500g. .... earth
Beef meatbones 5/8 oz / 200g. .... earth
Vinegar (Red wine vinegar) 1 dash / 3g. .... wood
Juniper berry 8 pieces / 6g. .... fire
Rosemary 1 pinch / 1g. .... fire
Carrot 3 pieces / 210g. .... earth
Parsnip 2 pieces / 300g. .... fire
Leek 1 piece / 200g. .... metal
Ginger fresh 1/2 teaspoon / 5g. .... metal
Lovage 1 stem / 15g. .... metal
Clove 2 pieces / 2g. .... metal
Pimento 6 pieces / 12g. .... metal
Anise (Common Fennel) 2 pieces / 1g. .... earth
Salt 1 teaspoon / 5g. .... water
Water 3,3 lbs / 1300g. .... earth

Cooking instructions:
Heat water, a dash of red wine vinegar, some juniper berries, a little rosemary, bones and meat till it boils; add carrot, parsnip, leek, ginger, lovage, clove, allspice, star anise and a little salt; simmer for 4-8 hours then strain.
Refrigerate for later use.

9.7 Basic recipe for a chicken broth worming

Strengthens Qi and blood, is very warm.
Cooking time approx. 2-3 hours
Calories p. portion: 90
9 portions
Allergens: L

Quantity of ingredients

Chicken meat 1/2 piece / 600g. .... wood
Carrot 2 pieces / 150g. .... earth
Leek 1 stick / 45g. .... metal
Celery root 1 piece / 500g. .... earth
Ginger fresh 2 slices / 2g. .... metal
Fenugreek (Trigonella foenum-graecum) 1 teaspoon / 2g. .... *
Juniper berry 1 teaspoon / 3g. .... fire
Bay leaf 3 pieces / 2g. .... *
Water 4 cup / 900g. .... earth

Cooking instructions:
Remove chicken parts from fat. Place chicken pieces in a saucepan with hot water and heat till it boils briefly, skimming any resulting foam. Add coarsely chopped vegetables and all spices and cook over medium heat for 2 to 3 hours. Strain the finished soup. Throw away vegetables and bones.
Tip: If you want to use the meat as a soup insert, take out after 45 minutes and return only the bones in the soup.
Refrigerate for later use.

9.8   Basic recipe for a duck broth

Forces Qi, strengthens blood and fluids, nourishes Yin, forces stomach, cools heat, strengthens spleen and liver.
Cooking time approx. 2-3 hours
Calories p. portion: 61
6 portions
Allergens: L

Quantity of ingredients
Duck (heart) 5/8 oz / 200g. .... wood
Water 2 cup / 450g. .... earth
Duck (slaughtered) 1/4 lbs - 4oz / 100g. .... wood
Carrot 2 pieces / 100g. .... earth
Celery root 1/2 piece / 600g. .... earth

Cooking instructions:
Cook duck pieces with vegetables for 2-3 hours. Sift broth through a fine sieve and refrigerate for later use.

The innards can be reused: You cut them finely and leaves them for a few minutes with fresh vegetables in the broth draw. Sprinkle with parsley before serving.

9.9   Basic recipe for a fish broth

Strengthens kidney Qi and Yin, strengthens blood and fluids, promotes urination.
Cooking time approx. 40 min
Calories p. portion: 128
5 portions
Allergens: DLO

Quantity of ingredients

Fish pieces mixed (fresh water) 3/4 lbs / 300g. ....water
Celery root 1/4 lbs - 4oz / 120g. .... earth
Leek 2 inches / 10g. ....metal
Carrot 2 pieces / 150g. .... earth
White wine 1/2 cup / 125g. .... wood
Lemon 1/2 piece / 50g. .... wood
Bay leaf 2 leaves / 2g. ....*
Peppercorns 3 pieces / 2g. ....metal
Olive oil 1 table spoon / 10g. .... earth
Water 2 cup / 450g. .... earth

Cooking instructions:

Fry celery, chopped carrots and leeks in olive oil, add bay leaf and peppercorns, add pieces of fish and sauté briefly. Add water, add little white wine or lemon. Simmer gently for 30 minutes. Skim off the resulting foam several times. In the end, sift the ingredients through a cloth. Refrigerate for later use.

9.10 Basic recipe for a reissue soup (Congee)

Warms the stomach and spleen, harmonizes the intestine, forces Qi, reduces moisture.
Cooking time approx. 2-4 hours
Calories p. portion: 140
3 portions

Quantity of ingredients

Rice variety any 1 cup / 120g. ....metal
Water 6 cups / 700g. .... earth

Cooking instructions:

Cook rice and water in a ratio of about 1: 6. The amount of water determines the thickness of the mash (matter of taste).
Put the rice in a saucepan with a heavy lid. It is important to simmer the rice after a short boil on the slightest flame, otherwise it burns.
Boil the rice for 2-4 hours. The longer he cooks, the more he strengthens.
If you want to eat the dish for breakfast, you can put the rice on just before bedtime.
To be on the safe side, you should first check the behavior of your pot and cooker under observation for a similar amount of time, so that nothing burns. Refrigerate for later use.

9.11 Basic recipe for a vegetable soup, nutritious

Strengthens spleen and lung, regulates Qi flow, builds up Qi, dries out, passes downwardly, strengthens stomach Qi.
Cooking time approx. 2-3 hours
Calories p. portion: 48
5 portions
Allergens: L

Quantity of ingredients

Olive oil 1 table spoon / 4g. .... earth
Onion white 1 piece / 60g. ....metal
Carrot 3 pieces / 200g. .... earth
Parsnip 3/8 lbs - 6oz / 150g. .... fire
Celery root 1 cup / 100g. .... earth
Ginger fresh 1/2 teaspoon / 2g. ....metal
Lemon 1/2 piece / 25g. ....wood
Juniper berry 6 pieces / 6g. .... fire
Thyme dried 1 pinch / 1g. ....metal
Lovage 1 table spoon / 3g. ....metal
Bay leaf 2 leaves / 1g. .... *
Salt 1 pinch / 1g. ....water
Water 3 cups / 650g. .... earth

Cooking instructions:

Cut the vegetables into cubes.
Heat oil in hot pot, fry shortly onions and vegetables.
Add cold water, then add ginger, bay leaf and lemon juice.
Season with juniper, thyme and lovage. Cover for 2 - 3 hours on a low heat and simmer.
The used vegetables should be thrown away.
The basic recipe serves as a soup base and to refine vegetables, legumes or cereals.
If you want to eat vegetable soup immediately, add the desired vegetables half an hour before.
Refrigerate for later use.

9.12 Black beans with avocado

Nourishing and slightly refreshing, builds up fluids, filling, nourishes Yin von liver, lungs and colon, moisturizes, relaxes, builds up Qi, spreads, forces stomach and kidney.
Cooking time approx. 1 hour
Calories p. portion: 264
3 portions
Allergens: EN

Quantity of ingredients

Black beans 1 cup / 100g. (recommended)................................water
Water 4 cups / 450g. (yes) .... earth
Lemon 1 dash / 1g. (recommended)...wood
Boxhorn clover seeds 1 pinch (powder) / 0,2g. ()..............................*
Sesame oil 1 table spoon / 10g. (yes).. earth
Ginger fresh 1 teaspoon / 2g. ()..metal
Wakame 1 inch / 1g. (yes)..water
Soy sauce 1 dash / 1g. (yes)...water
Avocado 1 piece / 300g. (recommended) .... earth

Cooking instructions:

Preparation the day before:
Soak 2 cups of black beans in about 6 cups of cold water for 6-8 hours and then strain.
Put the black beans in 4 cups of fresh cold water; add a dash of lemon juice, some fenugreek seed powder, 1 tablespoon of sesame oil, 1 teaspoon of grated ginger; add a piece of wakame or 1 tbsp of hijiki. Simmer for about 45 minutes; puree with the blender; season with plenty of soy sauce.

In the morning: Peel ½ avocado per serving and cut into small boats; Serve with the warm bean paste.

Note: The black beans can be pre-cooked for 2 - 3 days to be used as breakfast or other meals with little effort.

9.13 Celery juice

Strengthens stomach Qi, moisturizes, relaxes, builds up Qi, spreads.
Cooking time approx. 5 min
Calories p. portion: 33
1 portions
Allergens: L

Quantity of ingredients

Celery root 1/2 piece / 200g. (yes)... earth
Water 1 cup / 120g. (yes) .... earth
Salt 1 pinch / 0,5g. (recommended) ....water

Cooking instructions:

Peel celeriac and cut into pieces and juice. Mix with water and salt as needed.

9.14 Chicken soup with angelica root and buckthorn fruit

Strengthens spleen and nourishes the blood and Yin of the liver, forces Qi and blood, is very warming.
Cooking time approx. 1 1/2 hours
Calories p. portion: 77
3 portions
Allergens: LO

Quantity of ingredients

Basic recipe for a chicken soup (warming) 2 cup / 500g. (yes)..........*
Angelica root 1/8 oz / 5g. (recommended) ....*
Bocksdorn fruits, goji berry dried 1/8 lbs - 2oz / 50g. .... wood

Cooking instructions:

When you cook chicken broth according to basic recipes add angelica root and Bocksdorn fruits in the last 40 minutes.

Ingestion: Drink 2-3 cups of broth daily.

9.15 Compote from apples

Nourishes fluids, reduces stomach heat, forces spleen, produces essence, harmonizes stomach, warms the stomach and spleen, promotes blood circulation and conduction flow, relieves cold-sickness and pain.
Cooking time approx. 10 min
Calories p. portion: 67
2 portions

Quantity of ingredients
Apple (sweet) 1 piece / 220g. (yes) .... earth
Water 1 1/2 cups / 220g. (yes).. earth
Cinnamon ground 1 pinch / 1g. () .... *

Cooking instructions:
Cook the apples (organic) with the skin and seeds. Sprinkle with cinnamon.

9.16 Cooling rice dish with grapefruit

Lowers lung Qi, nourishes fluids, dissolves mucus, dries out, passes downwardly, warms the stomach and spleen, harmonizes the intestine, forces Qi, reduces moisture, strengthens Qi and Kidney Jing, moisturizes, relaxes, builds up Qi, spreads.
Cooking time approx. 20 min
Calories p. portion: 234
4 portions
Allergens: GHO

Quantity of ingredients
Rice round grain 1 cup / 120g. (yes)..metal
Water 5 cups / 600g. (yes) .... earth
Hazelnuts 2 table spoons / 20g. (yes).. earth
Raisins 2 table spoons / 20g. (little)... earth
Agave nectar 1 table spoon / 10g. (recommended)............................ *
Salt 1 pinch / 0,2g. (recommended)..water
Almond puree 1 table spoon / 10g. (little).................................. earth
Grapefruit (Pomelo) 1 piece / 200g. (yes) .... fire
Butter organic 2 teaspoons / 20g. (yes) .... earth

Cooking instructions:
Preparation on the eve: Pour round grain rice into cold water and cook. Soak chopped hazelnuts and raisins in some hot water overnight.

In the morning: Stir in a little hot water some agave syrup; add the rice and heat; add a small pinch of salt, almond paste, chopped grapefruit, the soaked chopped hazelnuts and raisins and mix; Serve with a small piece of butter.

9.17 Cous-Cous with date, coco and almondpuree

Forces Yin.
Cooking time approx. 10 min
Calories p. portion: 484
3 portions
Allergens: AHO

Quantity of ingredients
Couscous 1 1/2 cups / 240g. (little)..wood
Water 4 cups / 400g. (yes) .... earth
Dates dried 6 pieces / 20g. (little) .... earth
Coconut flakes 2 table spoons / 30g. (yes) .... earth
Almond puree 2 table spoons / 20g. (little)................................. earth
Olive oil 2 teaspoons / 20g. (yes).. earth
Apple (sweet) 1 piece grated / 120g. (yes)................................. earth
Vanilla 1 knife tip / 0,2g. (yes).. *

Cooking instructions:
Put couscous and olive oil in a large bowl and pour boiling water over them. Let it swell for 10 minutes. Crush dates and grate apple. Loosen up cous-cous with a fork. Mix in dates, coconut flakes, apple and almond paste.
Sweet to taste. Spices and flavors: vanilla, little chili

Winter variation: pear,
Summer variation: apricot, nectarine

9.18 Cream cheese substitute

Cools heat, keeps fluids, builds up blood and Yin.
Cooking time approx. 20 min
Calories p. portion: 526
2 portions
Allergens: AE

Quantity of ingredients

Soybean milk 4 cup / 300g. (recommended).............................. earth
Lemon 1 piece / 50g. (recommended) ....wood
Herbs various 2 table spoons / 6g. (recommended).......................... *
Whole grain bread 6 slices / 300g. (little) ....wood

Cooking instructions:

Heat the soy milk in a saucepan till it boils, stirring occasionally (gets burn easily!), Then allow to cool.
Squeeze out the lemon and stir gently under the cooled soy milk (approx. 80°C/176°F), let it approx. 20 min. rest or clot.
Pour chopped soy milk through a strainer lined with a dishcloth, allow liquid to drain and then squeeze out remaining liquid with the dishcloth.
Refine to taste with fresh herbs.
Serve with wholemeal bread.

9.19 Cucumber soup

Cools and moisturizes, diuretic, reduces damp heat, detoxifies, relaxes, builds up Qi, spreads, distributes mucus, passes downwardly, activates Wei Qi, forces Qi.
Cooking time approx. 20 min
Calories p. portion: 96
4 portions
Allergens: M

Quantity of ingredients

Olive oil 2 table spoons / 35g. (yes).. earth
Cucumber 2 pieces / 400g. (recommended) .... earth
Water 2 cup / 500g. (yes)... earth
Sage 3 leaves / 3g. (yes).. fire
Mustard 1/2 teaspoon / 0,5g. (recommended) ....metal
Coriander 1 pinch / 1g. (yes) ....metal
Cardamom 1 pinch / 1g. (recommended).. *
Salt 1 pinch / 1g. (recommended)..water

Cooking instructions:

Heat oil and roast short the small cucumbers. Add Mustard seeds, coriander, cardamom and salt. Add water. Simmer for 10-15 min. Puree and decorate with fresh chopped sage.

9.20 Duck with mung beans

Nourishes Yin, reduces heat, softens, passes downwardly, forces stomach und liver, regulates Qi flow,moisturizes, relaxes, spreads, dissolves stagnation.
Cooking time approx. 2 hours
Calories p. portion: 747
5 portions
Allergens: E

Quantity of ingredients
Duck (slaughtered) 1/2 piece / 1250g. (recommended).............. wood
Onion white 2 pieces / 120g. ()..metal
Carrot 1 piece / 120g. (yes).. earth
Garlic 1 clove / 3g. ()...metal
Mung bean 5/8 lbs - 8oz / 250g. (recommended)......................water
Peppercorns 3 pieces / 2g. ()...metal
Honey 1 teaspoon / 3g. (yes).. earth
Soy sauce 1 teaspoon / 3g. (yes) ....water
Lemon juice 1 teaspoon / 3g. (yes)...wood
Salt 1 pinch / 1g. (recommended)..water
Pepper (ground) 1 pinch / 0,5g. ()..metal
Olive oil 1 table spoon / 10g. (yes).. earth
Bay leaf 2 leaves / 2g. (recommended) .... *
Black caraway 1 pinch / 1g. (recommended) .... *
Savory 1 teaspoon / 2g. (recommended)...................................water

Cooking instructions:
The day before soak the mung beans and rinse the duck cold. Wash the vegetables, clean and cut into pieces. Put the duck and vegetables in a saucepan and cover with water. Add bay leaves, savory, mugwort and peppercorns. Boil over medium heat and simmer for 45 minutes. Skim off the foam. Remove duck from the stock, allow to cool and keep cool overnight.

In a saucepan, sauté the chopped onion in olive oil and pour in 1/4 liter of stock and add the pre-cooked vegetables. Add the mung beans and season with honey, soy sauce, lemon juice, salt, crushed black cumin and pepper.

Serve with rice or potatoes.

9.21 Italian champignon rice

Nourishes blood, moisturizes, relaxes, builds up Qi, spreads, wearms the stomach and spleen, harmonizes the intestine, forces Qi, reduces moisture, directs upwards, moisturizes, relaxes, builds up Qi, spreads.
Cooking time approx. 25 min
Calories p. portion: 256
4 portions
Allergens: G

Quantity of ingredients
Rice round grain 1 1/2 cups / 240g. (yes) ....metal
Water 2 cup / 450g. (yes)... earth
Pepper (ground) 1 pinch / 0,2g. ()...metal
Salt 1 pinch / 0,5g. (recommended)...water
Lemon juice 1 dash / 2g. (yes)...wood
Champignon 5/8 lbs - 8oz / 250g. (recommended).................... earth
Pepper powder (hot) 1 pinch / 0,2g. (recommended) .... fire
Olive oil 1 teaspoon / 3g. (yes) .... earth
Chives 1 teaspoon / 5g. () ....metal
Parmesan 2 table spoons / 20g. (little)...................................... earth

Cooking instructions:
Put the round grain rice in cold water 1:6 and cook.
Add ground pepper, salt, plenty of lemon juice, rose paprika, a little olive oil or butter and mix well.
Carefully add in mushrooms, chives or the green parts of the spring onion, and carefully add in some grated Parmesan cheese.
Goes well with vegetables and tofu dishes, tomato sauce dishes.

9.22 Kudzu soup in the morning

Moisturizes, relaxes, builds up Qi, spreads, forces stomach, harmonizes middle, reduces internal heat, detoxifies, softens, passes downwardly.
Cooking time approx. 5 min
Calories p. portion: 12
1 portions
Allergens: E

Quantity of ingredients
Water 1 cup / 250g. (yes) .... earth
Soy sauce 1 dash / 2g. (yes)..water
Umeboshi paste 1 knife tip / 2g. (recommended).......................water

Cooking instructions:
Mix kudzu with cold water and heat till it boils while stirring. Once it is glassy, remove from heat and let cool. Season with Tamari and Umeboshipaste or crushed umeboshi plums

There is always the possibility to support your stomach and intestines with this recipe, taken before the right breakfast.
A morning cure for stomach and mucous membranes. Fix the base balance.

9.23 Millet with egg and butter

Forces blood, Yin and Jing, nourishes Yin, moisturizes in case of internal dryness, forces blood, forces spleen, calms nerves and stomach, strengthens spleen and kidney, diuretic, strengthens Qi and kidney Jing, moisturizes, relaxes, builds up Qi, spreads.
Cooking time approx. 25 min
Calories p. portion: 338
2 portions
Allergens: CG

Quantity of ingredients
Millet 1 cup / 100g. (yes) .... earth
Ginger fresh 1/2 teaspoon / 1g. () .... metal
Salt 1 pinch / 0,5g. (recommended) .... water
Parsley 2 table spoons / 16g. (yes) .... wood
Pepper powder (hot) 1 pinch / 1g. (recommended) .... fire
Chicken egg 2 pieces / 100g. (yes) .... earth
Butter organic 2 table spoons / 20g. (yes) .... earth
Nutmeg 1 pinch / 0,2g. () .... metal
Water 1 1/2 cups / 200g. (yes) .... earth

Cooking instructions:
Simmer the millet with the ginger and nutmeg in the water for 5 min. and let it swell for another 30 min.
Cook and peel 1 soft egg per person; pile up the millet on plates and place 1 egg each in a hollow in the millet mountain; Put butterflakes over it. Sprinkle with chopped parsley and the rose paprika.

9.24 Pear compote

Moisturizes lungs, reduces lung mucus, nourishes lungs Qi.
Cooking time approx. 20 min
Calories p. portion: 100
3 portions

Quantity of ingredients
Water 1 1/2 cups / 240g. (yes)... earth
Pear 4 / 500g. (recommended)... earth

Cooking instructions:
Halve organic pears. Cores and skin can be used. Pear in the pot and add water. Simmer for up to 20 minutes until pears are tender.

9.25 Pear juice

Moisturizes lungs, reduces lung mucus, nourishes lungs Qi.
Cooking time approx. 5 min
Calories p. portion: 180
2 portions

Quantity of ingredients
Pear 3 pieces / 600g. (recommended).. earth

Cooking instructions:
Peel pears thinly (vitamins under the skin) and core. Juice in the juicer.

9.26 Quick flakes with compote or jam

Forces Qi, dries out, passes downwardly, strengthens middle heater, moisturizes, relaxes, builds up Qi, spreads, strengthens kidney Qi, essence and brain, forces kidney, warms the middle.
Cooking time approx. 5 min
Calories p. portion: 189
2 portions
Allergens: H

Quantity of ingredients
Quinoa 5-7 table spoons / 50g. (yes).. fire
Water 1 cup / 250g. (yes).. earth
Compote (fruits of the season) 1 cup / 100g. (recommended)...........*
Walnuts 1 table spoon (grated) / 8g. (little) .... earth
Olive oil 1 table spoon / 10g. (yes)... earth

Honey 2 table spoons / 20g. (yes) .... earth
Vanilla 1 pinch / 0,2g. (yes) .... *
Anise (Common Fennel) 1 pinch / 0,2g. () .... earth
Cardamom 1 pinch / 0,2g. (recommended) .... *

Cooking instructions:
Put the quinoa flakes in a pan and add water. Boil for 3-5 minutes, pull
from the fire, add nuts and compote. Add a dash of oil. Sweeten as
needed with honey, whole cane sugar or agave syrup.

Spices and aromas: vanilla, anise, fennel or coriander, cardamom, a
little chili.

Winter: apple compote, pear compote, fruit jam.
Summer: plum compote, apricot compote.

9.27 Radish with horseradish

Slightly refreshing and moisturizing, dissolves stagnation, nourishes
blood and liver, harmonizes liver and spleen, forces eyesight, preserves
the fluids, contracts, nourishes the lungs and spleen, distributes mucus,
dissolves mucus, dissolves stagnation, directs upwards.
Cooking time approx. 30 min
Calories p. portion: 196
2 portions
Allergens: GNO

Quantity of ingredients
Butter organic 1 table spoon / 8g. (yes) .... earth
Radish (white, green, purple-red) 1/2 piece / 50g. (yes) .... metal
Water 2 table spoons / 10g. (yes) .... earth
Lemon juice 2 table spoons / 20g. (yes) .... wood
White wine 2 table spoons / 20g. () .... wood
Pepper powder (hot) 1 pinch / 0,2g. (recommended) .... fire
Sesame oil 1 teaspoon / 3g. (yes) .... earth
Radish horseradish 2 table spoons / 20g. (recommended) .... metal
Salt 1 pinch / 0,5g. (recommended) .... water
Parsley 1 Bunch (chopped) / 80g. (yes) .... wood
Rice long grain rice 1/2 cup / 60g. (recommended) .... metal
Water 3 cups / 300g. (yes) .... earth
Salt 1 pinch / 0,5g. (recommended) .... water

Cooking instructions:
In a hot pan melt the butter, sautéed into stripes cut radish. Add cold water, lemon juice, white wine, a pinch of rose paprika and stir in the sesame oil; with 2 - 3 tablespoons fresh grated horseradish (alternatively 1 teaspoon from the glass), salt to taste; Sprinkle with chopped parsley.

Place the rice with the water, salt and cook for about 15 minutes.

9.28 Red lentils with avocado and radish

Nutritious and moisturizing builds up Qi and fluids, drives sweat, reduces blood fat, stimulates, dissolves stagnation.
Cooking time approx. 20 min
Calories p. portion: 269
3 portions
Allergens: N

Quantity of ingredients
Ginger fresh 2 slices / 2g. () .... metal
Water 1 1/2 cups / 200g. (yes).. earth
Lentils red 1 cup peeled / 100g. (yes)..water
Wakame 1 inch / 1g. (yes)..water
Salt 1 pinch / 0,5g. (recommended)..water
Lemon juice 1 dash / 1g. (yes)...wood
Curcuma 1 pinch / 0,3g. ()...*
Avocado 1 piece / 300g. (recommended) .... earth
Pepper (ground) 1 pinch / 0,2g. ()...metal
Pepper powder (hot) 1 pinch / 0,2g. (recommended) .... fire
Sesame oil 1 dash / 1g. (yes)... earth
Radish (white, green, purple-red) 1 cup / 100g. (yes)................metal

Cooking instructions:
Put in a pot with water, some chopped ginger, peeled red lentils, a piece of wakame or a small amount of hijiki and simmer until the lentils are soft. Season with salt, lemon juice and turmeric.

Meanwhile: place half an avocado per serving on one-third of the plate: add ground pepper, a pinch of salt, a little lemon juice, a pinch of sweet pepper and a little sesame oil.
Put the grated radish on the second plate third.
Fill the lentil dish into the last third of the plate.
Variant: Use radish slices instead of radishes.

9.29 Refreshing cucumber soup with potatoes

Reduces damp heat, detoxifies, forces Qi, forces spleen, relieves inflammation, spreads.
Cooking time approx. 15 min
Calories p. portion: 148
3 portions
Allergens: GN

Quantity of ingredients
Sesame oil 1 table spoon / 10g. (yes).. earth
Potato 4 pieces / 300g. (recommended) .... earth
Onion (spring onion) 3 pieces / 60g. ()..metal
Pepper (ground) 1 pinch / 0,5g. ()...metal
Nutmeg 1 pinch / 1g. ()...metal
Salt 1 pinch / 1g. (recommended)..water
Lemon 1/2 piece / 25g. (recommended) .... wood
Cucumber 2 pieces / 500g. (recommended) .... earth
Cream, sweet 30% 1 table spoon / 10g. (little).................................*
Dill 1 table spoon / 15g. (little) ....metal

Cooking instructions:
Sauté sesame oil, chopped potatoes, plenty of spring onions in a hot pot; add pepper, a little nutmeg, salt, lemon juice, hot water, diced cucumber; simmer for about 10 minutes and then puree; add some sweet cream as you like, fresh dill.

Variation: Add a little chili, oregano, thyme or rosemary to soften the cooling effect.

9.30 Reissue soup with duck

Nourishes Yin, warms the stomach and spleen, harmonizes the intestine, forces Qi, reduces moisture,nourishes blood and liver, harmonizes liver and spleen, moisturizes, relaxes, builds up Qi, spreads.
Cooking time approx. 1 1/2 hours
Calories p. portion: 161
6 portions
Allergens: EG

Quantity of ingredients

Rice round grain 1 cup / 100g. (yes)...metal
Water 8 cups / 900g. (yes) .... earth
Duck (slaughtered) 5/8 lbs - 8oz / 250g. (recommended)...........wood
Shiitake, dried 4-6 pieces / 5g. (yes)... earth
Parsley 2 table spoons / 12g. (yes)...wood
Butter organic 1 teaspoon / 3g. (yes).. earth
Soy sauce 1 dash / 2g. (yes)...water

Cooking instructions:

Soak shiitake mushrooms. Prepare rice soup according to the basic
recipe. Add duck meat and shiitake mushrooms for the last 30 minutes.
Add oyster mushrooms, parsley and a little butter at the very end.
Season with soy sauce.

Variant: Add soaked and cooked adzuki beans. They enhance the
diuretic effect.

9.31 Rice congee with honey pear and black sesame

Especially good in kidney Yin deficiency, moisturizes lungs, cools heat,
reduces lung mucus, produces humors, moisturizes, relaxes, builds up
Qi, spreads, moisturizes intestines, nourishes Yin.
Cooking time approx. 10 min - 3 hours
Calories p. portion: 158
2 portions
Allergens: N

Quantity of ingredients

Basic recipe for a rice soup (Congee) 1 1/2 cups / 240g. (yes)..........*
Pear 2 pieces / 300g. (recommended).. earth
Sesame, black 1 teaspoon / 3g. (recommended).......................wood

Cooking instructions:

Cook rice congee according to basic recipe.
Fill pot with 3 cm of water and heat till it boils. Quarter the pears (with
the skin and seeds) and simmer them covered with black sesame for 10
minutes. Mix with the rice.

9.32 Rice congee with mung beans

Warms the stomach and spleen, harmonizes the intestine, forces Qi, reduces moisture, reduces heat, softens, passes downwardly, moisturizes, laxative, antiparasitic.
Cooking time approx. 2 hours
Calories p. portion: 424
2 portions

Quantity of ingredients
Basic recipe for a rice soup (Congee) 4 cups / 500g. (yes) .... *
Mung bean 1/2 cup / 50g. (recommended) .... water
Herbs various 2 table spoons / 8g. (recommended) .... *
Rapeseed oil 2 table spoons / 20g. (yes) .... earth

Cooking instructions:
Soak the mung beans the day before and strain. Cook the rice according to the basic recipe and cook the mung beans with the rice.

Finally, add fresh herbs and a dash of high-quality cold-pressed oil.

9.33 Rice dulse soup

Strengthens spleen and liver, regulates Qi flow, relaxes, builds up Qi, spreads, dries out, passes downwardly, strengthens stomach Qi, warms the stomach and spleen, harmonizes the intestine, forces Qi, reduces moisture.
Cooking time approx. 5 min
Calories p. portion: 190
2 portions
Allergens: L

Quantity of ingredients
Basic recipe for a rice soup (Congee) 4 cups / 500g. (yes) .... *
Basic recipe for a vegetable soup (nutritious) 2 cup / 500g. (recommended)*
Dulse (seaweed) 2 table spoons / 15g. (recommended) .... water

Cooking instructions:
Worm up a portion of pre-cooked basic recipe for a ricesoupe (congee) and a portion pre-cooked basic recipe for a vegetable soup.
Bake the dulse in the oven at 220 degrees for 3 minutes. Spread the crisp dulse over the rice.

9.34 Rice porridge with orange peel

Warms the stomach and spleen, harmonizes the intestine, forces Qi, reduces moisture. brings the Liver Qi in motion, cools heat, moisturizes, relaxes, builds up Qi, spreads. nourishes blood, moisturizes, relaxes, builds up Qi, spreads.
Cooking time approx. 10 min
Calories p. portion: 120
4 portions
Allergens: L

Quantity of ingredients
Rice variety any 1 cup / 100g. (yes)...metal
Water 6 cups / 600g. (yes) .... earth
Orange grated peel 1/4 piece / 3g. (recommended)...........................*
Olive oil 1 table spoon / 10g. (yes)... earth
Champignon 1/2 cup / 50g. (recommended)............................... earth
Celery sticks 1/2 bunch / 60g. (recommended) .... earth
Basic recipe for a chicken soup 3-4 table spoons / 40g. (yes)............*
Salt 1 pinch / 0,5g. (recommended)..water

Cooking instructions:
The day before boil the rice with the orange peel and water in a ratio of about 1: 6. The amount of water determines the thickness of the mash (pure matter of taste). Put the rice in a saucepan with good insulation and a heavy lid. It is important to simmer the rice after a short boil on the slightest flame, otherwise it burns. Boil the rice for 2-4 hours. The longer he cooks, the more he strengthens.
Heat the oil in a saucepan, add the chopped champignon and celery and sauté briefly. Add the rice. Add vegetable broth or water, warm up, salt.

9.35 Rice with stewed vegetables

Dissipates heat and moisture.
Cooking time approx. 20 min
Calories p. portion: 166
2 portions
Allergens: L

Quantity of ingredients

Rice variety any 1/2 cup / 60g. (yes)...metal
Water 3 cups / 300g. (yes) .... earth
Lemon peel 1 piece / 3g. (yes) .... fire
Water 1/2 cup / 0g. (yes).. earth
Carrot 2 pieces / 180g. (yes) .... earth
Celery sticks 1/2 piece / 5g. (recommended) .... earth
Champignon 1/2 cup / 50g. (recommended)................................ earth
Cress 2 table spoons / 20g. (recommended) ....metal
Linseed oil 1 dash / 3g. (yes).. earth

Cooking instructions:

Cook rice according to basic recipe with a piece of lemon peel.
Steam chopped carrots, celery and mushrooms until soft.
Then sprinkle with cress. Then add a dash of high quality cold oil.

9.36 Roasted millet with Celery sticks

Strengthens spleen and kidney, diuretic, brings the liver Qi in motion,
cools heat, moisturizes, relaxes, builds up Qi, spreads.
Cooking time approx. 30 min
Calories p. portion: 400
2 portions
Allergens: L

Quantity of ingredients

Millet 1 cup / 120g. (yes) .... earth
Water 1 1/2 cups / 240g. (yes)... earth
Celery sticks 2 rods / 50g. (recommended)............................... earth
Water 2 table spoons / 30g. (yes).. earth
Herbs various 1 table spoon / 10g. (recommended)........................*
Salt 1 pinch / 1g. (recommended)...water
Sage 3-4 leaves / 2g. (yes).. fire
Cress 1 teaspoon / 3g. (recommended)...................................metal

Cooking instructions:

Roast millet briefly, pour over water, heat till it boils and let stand for 20
min. to swell.

Cut celery into small pieces and mix with water, salt and fresh herbs
and cook for 10 min. Add to the millet. Sprinkle fresh sage or
watercress over it.

9.37 Spinach with Tahini

Nourishes blood and Yin, forces Zang-organs, forces stomach and intestines, harmonizes Qi, moisturizes lungs, forces Qi, forces spleen, relieves inflammation, moisturizes, relaxes, builds up Qi, spreads, nourishes blood.
Cooking time approx. 20 min
Calories p. portion: 150
4 portions
Allergens: N

Quantity of ingredients

Potato 1,1 lbs / 500g. (recommended).. earth
Salt 1 pinch / 0,2g. (recommended)...water
Water 1 cup / 25g. (yes)... earth
Spinach 2,2 lbs / 800g. (recommended) .... earth
Sesame paste (Tahini) 2 table spoons / 20g. (recommended) ... earth

Cooking instructions:

Cook potatoes and peel. Heat water. Blanch spinach. Shake off water and let it dry and stir with sesame.

9.38 Strawberry soup with melons

Forces blood, cools blood, preserves the fluids, contracts, moisturizes, spreads, forces heart Yin.
Cooking time approx. 5 min
Calories p. portion: 87
2 portions

Quantity of ingredients

Strawberries 3/4 lbs / 300g. (yes) ....wood
Strawberry Juice 1/3 cup / 70g. (yes)..wood
Lemon peel 1/4 teaspoon / 1g. (yes)... fire
Cantaloupe 5/8 oz / 200g. (recommended)................................ earth

Cooking instructions:

Puree strawberries (fresh or frozen) and strawberry juice with the blender, mix in a little sugar.
Cut melon pulp into small pieces.
Arrange strawberry soup in portions. Put the melon cubes in the sweet soup.

9.39 Tea from celery sticks

Brings the Liver Qi in motion, cools heat, moisturizes, relaxes, builds up Qi, spreads.
Cooking time approx. 15 min
Calories p. portion: 1
4 portions
Allergens: L

Quantity of ingredients
Celery sticks 2 table spoons (chopped) / 18g. (recommended) .. earth
Water 2 cup / 500g. (yes) .... earth

Cooking instructions:
Heat the water till it boils and put it aside. Add cutted celery and cook for 10 min. to let go. Strain. Sweet to taste with honey.

9.40 Tea from Melissa

Preserves the fluids, contracts, soothes liver fire, stimulates lungs Qi.
Cooking time approx. 10 min
Calories p. portion: 0
4 portions

Quantity of ingredients
Balm 2 teaspoons / 4g. (recommended) .... wood
Water 2 cup / 500g. (yes) .... earth

Cooking instructions:
Heat the water till it boils and put it aside. Add lemon balm and 10 min. to let go. Sweet to taste with honey. Strain when pouring.

9.41 Tea Green tea

Reduces internal heat, dissolves mucus, detoxifies.
Cooking time approx. 10 min
Calories p. portion: 2
1 portions

Quantity of ingredients
Green tea 1 teaspoon / 2g. (recommended) .... fire
Water 1 cup / 120g. (yes) .... earth

Cooking instructions:

For each cup you use a teaspoonful or a teabag.

Pour green tea only with 60 to 80 ° C / 140 to 176 °F hot water, otherwise it will be bitter.

If the tea has a stimulating effect, let it draw for two to three minutes. It has a calming effect for a duration of five minutes (no longer, otherwise it will be bitter!).

Another method: Pour the tea leaves with about 70 ° C / 158 °F hot water and pour the water immediately again. Then just pour hot water again. The bitter substances disappear and the tea gets a milder aroma.

9.42 Vegetable porridge

Strengthens spleen and liver, regulates Qi flow, moisturizes, relaxes, builds up Qi, distributes, relieves inflammation, strengthens Qi, blood and Jing and middle heat, strengthens essence, preserves the fluids, pulls together.

Cooking time approx. 20 min
Calories p. portion: 161
1 portions
Allergens: G

Quantity of ingredients

Potato 1 piece / 50g. (recommended)... earth
Carrot (Early Carrot) 1/4 lbs - 4oz / 100g. (yes).......................... earth
Chicken meat 1 oz / 30g. (little) ....wood
Butter organic 1 table spoon / 10g. (yes) .... earth

Cooking instructions:

Wash the potato and put it unpeeled in a small pot. Cover with a little water and bring to boil, then cook the potatoes on a low heat for 15-20 minutes.

Meanwhile, wash the carrots, clean, peel and cut into pieces about 2 cm in size. Steam with 3 tablespoons of water and the meat in a pot for about 15 minutes.

Finely chop the carrots and meat with a blender. Add the butter and puree everything.

(Change again and again the vegetables: kohlrabi, zucchini, parsnips)

9.43 Vegetable semolina soup

Strengthens spleen and liver, regulates Qi flow, builds up Qi, dries out, passes downwardly, reduces moisture, regulates Qi.
Cooking time approx. 20 min
Calories p. portion: 199
3 portions
Allergens: AEGL

Quantity of ingredients
Basic recipe for a vegetable soup 2 cup / 500g. (recommended) .... *
Potato 1 piece / 80g. (recommended)... earth
Parsnip 1 piece / 180g. (yes).. fire
Carrot 1 piece / 120g. (yes).. earth
Celery root 3/8 lbs - 6oz / 150g. (yes)... earth
Kohlrabi 1/2 piece / 200g. (yes).. earth
Beans (green, fresh) 1/4 lbs / 100g. (recommended) .... water
Wheat semolina 2 table spoons / 24g. (yes) .... wood
Lovage 1/2 teaspoon / 2g. (yes) .... metal
Butter organic 1 table spoon / 20g. (yes) .... earth
Soy sauce 1 teaspoon / 3g. (yes) .... water

Cooking instructions:
Worm the prepared vegetable soup; cook the vegetables in the soup softly. Spread some wheatgrass and let it swell. At the end, add lovage-green and a little butter and taste with soy sauce.

9.44 Wheat fresh grain porridge with pears.

Moisturizes lungs, cools heat, reduces lung mucus, nourishes Yin from heart and kidney, forces heart and kidney, moisturizes, relaxes, builds up Qi, spreads.
Cooking time approx. 25 min
Calories p. portion: 309
2 portions
Allergens: ANO

Quantity of ingredients
Wheat 1 cup / 100g. (yes) .... wood
Water 2-4 cups / 350g. (yes) .... earth
Pear 2 pieces / 300g. (recommended)...................................... earth
Raisins 1 table spoon / 10g. (little).. earth
Sesame, white 1 table spoon / 8g. (recommended) .... earth
Sunflower seeds 1 table spoon / 8g. (yes) .... earth

Cardamom 1 pinch / 0,3g. (recommended)..*
Salt 1 pinch / 0,3g. (recommended)..water

Cooking instructions:
Preparation the night before: Wheat roughly cut; soak overnight.

In the morning: Put the wheat meal with a little hot water; simmer with stirring for about 15 minutes.
Meanwhile, add pear compote, raisins, crushed sesame, sunflower seeds, some ground cardamom, a small pinch of salt.

Variants: with grated apple or seasonal fruit.

10 Effects of food

10.1 Use ingredients: recommendable

Acai powder
Acerola fruit nectar or powder
Agave nectar
Agrimony
Almond
Aloe juice
Amaranth Pops
Anchovy / Sardine
Angelica root
Apple puree
Apricot dried
Apricot jam
Apricot nectar
Apricots juice
Avocado
Baking powder
Balm
Banchatee (green tea)
barberry
Barley
Barley flour
Barley grass powder
Barley malt
Barley not peeled
Basic recipe for a beef soup
Basic recipe for a beef soup (warming)
Basic recipe for a duck soup
Basic recipe for a fish soup
Basic recipe for a vegetable soup
(nutritious)
Batavia
Bay leaf
Beans (green, fresh)
Bearberry leaf
Beef bone marrow
Beef heart
Beef heart (calf)
Beef kidney
Beef lungs (calf)
Beef Oxtail pieces
Beef soup meat
Beer (alcohol-free)
Beer (alcohol-reduced)
Berries of the season
Berry juice
Bitter Herb liqueur
Bitter Lemon
Bitter liqueur
Bitter orange peel

Black beans
Black caraway
Black fungus mushroom
Blackberry dried (unripe fruit)
Blackberry jam
Blackberry leaves
Blackthorn (Sloe)
Blue mallow tee
Blueberry dried
Blueberry jam
Bocksdorn fruits (Fructus Lycii, Goji,
goji berry dried
Borage
Brazil nuts
Brown ale
Buckbean
Bush beans
Butter beans white
Calamari
Campari
Cantaloupe
Capers in olive oil
Cardamom
Carob flour, St. john's bread
Carp
Celery sticks
Chamomile
Chamomile tea
Champignon
Channa-Dal
Chenpi (chinese tangerine bowl)
Cherry (sour)
Cherry compote
Chervil
Chervil dried
Chestnut puree
Chicken Blood
Chicken egg white
Chicken heart
Chicken liver
Chicken stomach
Chicken yolk
Chickweed
Chicory
Chinese cabbage
Chinese pearl barley
Chocolate (Diabetic)
Chrysanthemum blossom tea
Clarified butter

Clementine
Coconut fat
Coconut meat
Cod
Codfish
Cola drink
Cola drink (low calorie)
Compote (fruits of the season)
Coriander (fresh)
Corn germ oil
Corn Grease (Polenta)
Corn silk tea
Corn starch
Cranberries
Cranberry
Cranberry jam
Cream 10% coffee cream
Creamer
Cress
Crucian
Cucumber
Cucumber (bitter)
Cucumber (spicy cucumber)
Currant jam (black)
Currant jam (red)
Currant juice (black)
Currants (black)
Currants (red)
Curry paste red
Daisy
Dandelion juice
Dashi
Dates red
Deer's Bones
Deer's kidneys
Duck (heart)
Duck (slaughtered)
Ducks egg
Dulse (seaweed)
Dyer's broom herb
Eel smoked
Elderberries
Endive salad
Fennel seeds ground
Fenugreek (Trigonella foenum-graecum)
Fernet Branca (herbal bitter liqueur)
Fish innards
Fish pieces mixed (fresh water)
Fish remains
Fish sauce
Flounder
Flower pollen
Fox nut, gorgon nut, makhana

Fresh cheese from soya
Freshwater crab
Freshwater fish
Fructose (glucose)
Fruit mix juice
Fruit tea
Gail plum
Galangal
Garam Masala powder
Gelatin white
Gelee Royal
Gentian root
Gentian root tea
Ginger oil
Ginkgo fruit
Ginseng
Ginseng liqueur
Ginseng root
Goat and sheep's blood
Goat and sheep's brain
Goat and sheep's liver
Goat and sheep's stomach
Goose
Goose blood
Goose egg
Goose fat
Goose parts
Grapefruit dried peel
Grapeseed oil
Grass carp
Green tea
Greengage
Ground
Ground caraway
Guava
Halibut (Flatfish)
Hawthorn
Herbal tea mix
Herbs of Provence
Herbs various
Herbs wild
Herring
Hibiscus
Hibiscus tea
Hijiki
Hokkaido pumpkin
Honey wine (Met)
Hop
Horehound leaves
Horse meat
Jasmine blossoms tee
Jellyfish
Kaki plum
Kalmus

Kidney beans (red)
King Solomon's-seal
Kudzu
Kukicha tea
Ladyfingers
Lamb bones
Lamb kidneys
Lamb liver
Lamb shoulder
Lavender blossoms
Leaf salads (bitter)
Lemon
Lemon Balm (dried)
Lemon Balm (fresh)
Lemongrass
Lettuce
Licorice root tea
Lily bulbs
Lima beans
Lime blossom tea
Liver smoothing tea
Loquate / Japanese medlar
Lotus roots
Lotus seeds
Lovage seeds
Luo Han Guo fruit
Lychee liqueur
Mackerel
Mango juice
Martini
Mascarpone cheese
Mayonnaise 50%
Mayonnaise 80%
Mediterranean fish (cod, plaice,
haddock, sea eel, mackerel)
Medlar
Mineral water
Mirabelle plum
Miso black (fermented)
Mixed Pickles
Mu Erh Mushroom
Muesli
Mulled Wine Spice
Mullet
Mung bean
Mung bean sprouting
Mustard
Mustard Dijon
Mustard medium hot
Mustard sweet
Nasturtium (nose-twister or nose-
tweaker)
Nectarine
Nettles

Nori, purple seaweed, red algae
Octopus
Olives green
Orange blossom
Orange dried peel
Orange grated peel
Orange jam
Orange peel
Oregano fresh
Oyster shell powder
Oysters
Palm oil
Parsley root
Passion blossoms tea
Passion fruit
Peanut (roasted)
Peanut butter
Pear
Pearl barley
Pepper powder (hot)
Peppermint
Peppermint tea
Pepperoni
Pepperoni, red, pitted, halved
Pepperoni, yellow, pitted, halved
Peppers (sweet)
Peppers powder
Perch
Pig blood
Pigeon
Pigeon egg
Pinto beans speckled
Plaice
Plum dried
Plums
Pork Bacon
Pork brain
Pork fat (lard)
Pork ham
Pork ham cooked
Pork ham smoked
Pork heart
Pork kidneys
Pork knuckle
Pork Lard
Pork liver
Pork lung
Pork marrow bones
Pork meat
Pork sausage (Bratwurst) Pork skin
Pork stomach
Pork/beef sausage (smoked)
Pork's intestine
Potato

Potato (mealy)
Potato flour
Prickly pear
Prosecco
Psyllium seed
Pudding powder vanilla
Puff pastry
Quail
Quail egg
Rabbit (wild)
Rabbit liver
Rabbit meat
Radicchio
Radish horseradish
Radish leaves
Raspberry jam
Raspberry leaf tea
Red beet
Reishi mushroom
Ribworttea
Rice long grain rice
Rose blossom tea
Rose hip
Rose hip tea
Rose leaf tea
Rosefish
Rucola
Rum
Safflower (Dyer's thistle / Hong Hua)
Salmon
Salt
Salt (herbal)
Savory
Sea buckthorn
Sea cucumber
Sesame oil roasted
Sesame paste (Tahini)
Sesame, black
Sesame, white
Shark
Sherry (whine)
Shrimps
Slug
Soy flour
Soy noodles
Soy Tofu
Soy Tofu smoked
Soya Cuisine (soy cream)
Soybean milk
Soybeans
Soybeans, blacks, fermented
Spelled (Dark) bread
Spelled grain

Spelled wholemeal flour
Spinach
Spurdog (spiny dogfish, Schillerlocken)
St. Benedict's thistle, blessed thistle,
holy thistle, spotted thistle
Stevia (candyleaf, sweetleaf)
Strawberry jam
Sugar - icing sugar
Sugar molasses
Sugar palm sugar
Sugar substitute (sweetener)
Supplementary nutrition
Tabasco
Tea mixture uric acid lowering
Thyme dried
Tomato dried
Tomato juice
Tomato paste
Tomato puree
Tonic Water
Trout
Trout (smoked)
Truffle
Tuna
Turkey ham
Turmeric (yellow root)
Turnip
Umeboshi paste
Valerian
Vanilla pod
Vanilla sugar natural
Vinegar Aceto Balsamico white
Walnut oil
Watermelon
Wax gourd
Wheatgrass juice
Wheatgrass powder
Whitefish
Wild garlic (garlic spinach)
Wild herbs
Wild strawberries
Wormwood
Wormwood herb
Yam root, yam root tuber
Yarrow
Yeast
Yew nut
Zucchini

10.2 Use ingredients: yes

Adzuki beans
Agar agar (kelp)
Amaranth
Apple (sweet)
Apple juice (natural cloudy)
Arrowroot
Artichoke
Asparagus (green or white)
Aubergine
Bamboo shoots
Barley grouts
Basic recipe for a chicken soup (warming)
Basic recipe for a rice soup (Congee)
Beef liver
Beer (Pils)
Beer (Top-fermented German dark beer)
Black tea
Blackberry´s
Black-eyed peas
Boletus mushroom
Borage oil
Bread roll
Bread with carob kernel flour
Breadcrumbs (wheat bread, bread roll)
Broad beans (thick beans)
Broccoli
Brussels sprouts
Buckwheat
Buckwheat (roasted) Kasha
Buckwheat whole grain
Burdock root tea
Butter organic
Carambola (Star fruit)
Carrot
Carrot (Early Carrot)
Carrot juice without sugar
Cashews
Cauliflower
Caviar
Celery root
Chanterelle
Chard
Chicken egg
Chickpeas
Chlorella (fresh water)
Coconut flakes
Coconut grated
Coix (seeds) YiYi Ren
Cooking oil

Coriander
Corn
Crab
Crispbread
Dandelion (young plants)
Dandelionroots tea
Elderberry blossom tee
Evening primrose oil
Fig
Fig dried
Gourd
Grape juice red
Grape juice white
Grapefruit (Pomelo)
Grapefruit juice
Grapes red
Grapes white
Hazelnuts
Herbs bitter
Honey
Iceberg lettuce
Kohlrabi
Kombu seaweed (Saccharina japonica)
Lamb's lettuce
Lamb's lettuce
Lemon juice
Lemon peel
Lentils
Lentils black
Lentils red
Lentils yellow
Lime
Linseed oil
Lovage
Lychee
Lychee in Preserved
Malt
Mango
Manioc flour
Maple syrup
Margarine
Margarine (diet)
Millet
Millet flakes
Miso
Miso paste (soy bean paste)
Morel (black, dried)
Morel, dried
Mulberry fruit
Mussels
Octopus

Olive oil
Olives
Parsley
Parsnip
Peanut oil
Peanuts
Peas
Peas, green
Pine nuts
Pistachios
Plum
Pumpkin
Pumpkin seed oil
Pumpkin seeds
Quince
Quinoa
Radish
Radish (white, green, purple-red)
Radish black
Rapeseed oil
Red cabbage
Rice (Gaoliang / Sorghum)
Rice (whole grain)
Rice Basmati
Rice black
Rice flour
Rice mash
Rice red
Rice round grain
Rice starch
Rice sticky
Rice variety any
Rice wild (nature rice)
Romaine lettuce / lettuce salad
Rusk
Rye
Rye flour
Saffron
Sage
Salsify
Savoy cabbage / kale
Seacrab
Sesame oil
Shiitake, dried
Soy sauce
Soybean oil
Soybeans, black
Soybeans, yellow
Spelled flakes
Strawberries
Strawberry Juice

Sugar candy white
Sugar cane sugar
Sugar fructose - fruit sugar
Sugar glucose - grapes sugar
Sugar Milk Sugar
Sugar white
Sunflower oil
Sunflower seeds
Sweet potato
Tarragon (Estragon)
Thistle oil
Tomato
Topinambur
Turnips
Vanilla
Vanilla powder
Vegetable juice
Wakame
Water
Water hot
Wheat
Wheat beer
Wheat bran
Wheat bulgur
Wheat flakes
Wheat flatbread/pita bread
Wheat flour
Wheat flour whole grain
Wheat germ oil
Wheat semolina
Wheat semolina for children
Wheat/Rye/Gray-black bread with yeast
White beans
White bread (baguette)
White bread (pretzel sticks)
White bread (roll)
White bread (wheat bread)
White breadcrumbs
White cabbage
White dumpling bread (wheat bread cut into chunks)
Wholemeal flour
Yarrow tea
Yogurt (natural, 1.5% fat)
Yogurt (natural, 3.5% fat)

10.3 Use ingredients: little

Almond marzipan
Almond milk
Almond puree
Apple (sour)
Apricot
Apricots
Banana
Banana (cooking banana)
Beef fillet
Beef meat
Beef meat (calf)
Beef meatbones
Beef stomach
Blueberry
Blueberry juice
Bulgur (cereals)
Butter (half fat)
Buttermilk
Camembert
Chestnuts
Chicken meat
Clementines
Coconut milk
Corn (fast polenta)
Corn (roasted)
Corn flour
Cottage cheese
Couscous
Cow's milk (1.5% fat)
Cow's milk (whole milk 3.5% fat)
Cranberry
Cranberry juice
Cream (30% fat)
Cream sour 10%
Cream sour 20%
Cream, sweet 30%
Créme fraiche cheese
Curd cheese 20%
Curd cheese 40%
Currant (black)
Currant (red)
Currant (white)
Dates dried
Dill
Edam cheese
Eel
Emmental cheese
Fennel
Feta cheese
French beans

Fresh cheese
Fresh cheese with herbs
Gooseberry
Gouda cheese
Kefir
Linseed
Linseed (crushed)
Longane
Lye roll
Mallow (Malva sylvestris) blossom tea
Mare's milk
Mozzarella
Multi-grain bread (gray bread)
Noodles (wheat) with egg
Noodles (wheat, lasagne) with egg
Noodles (wheat, ribbon noodles) with egg
Noodles (wheat, spaghetti) with egg
Noodles (whole grain) with egg
Okra
Oyster mushroom
Parmesan
Pear juice
Pearl barley
Peppers
Pimento
Pineapple
Pineapple (from a can)
Pineapple juice without sugar
Processed cheese 12%
processed cheese 30%
Rabbit
Raisins
Raspberry
Raspberry dried (immature)
Red berry (without sugar)
Rice (fragrance)
Rice malt
Rice noodles
Rice sweet
Rye wholemeal bread
Sago (cereals)
Skim milk powder
Spelled semolina
Sugar brown
Tangerine
Toast bread (whole grain)
Tsampa (roasted barley flour)
Turkey breast meat
Walnuts

Whey
Whole grain bread

Yoghurt vanilla

10.4 Do not use contra-acting foods

Anise (Common Fennel)
Basil
Basil (fresh)
Bean oil
Boxhorn clover seeds
Brie cheese
Cereal coffee
Cherry
Cherry juice
Chili (pod or ground)
Chives
Chocolate
Cinnamon ground
Cinnamon sticks
Clove
Cocoa
Coffee
Cream sour 30%
Cumin (Caraway seed)
Curcuma
Curry
Deer meat
Deer meat
Fennel tea
Feta cheese
Garlic
Ginger fresh
Ginger powder
Goat
Goat and sheep's milk
Goat cheese
Gorgonzola
Green spelt
Hyssop
Juniper berry
Kiwi
Kumquats
Lamb meat
Leek
Lobster
Marjoram
Mold cheese
Mustard seeds
Mutton
Mutton
Nutmeg
Oat
Oat flakes (whole grain)
Oat flakes roasted

Oat flour
Oat fusion (baby food)
Oat meal
Oat milk
Onion (shallot)
Onion (spring onion)
Onion read
Onion white
Orange
Orange juice
Oregano dried
Papaya
Peaches
Peaches (canned)
Pepper (ground)
Pepper Cayenne
Pepper white (ground)
Peppercorns
Peppers (rose peppers)
Pheasant
Pickle
Pomegranate
Poppy
Pumpernickel (dark bread)
Red wine
Rhubarb
Rosemary
Sake
Sauerkraut (cutted cabbage fermented)
Sheep's milk yoghurt
Shrimp
Sorrel
Sour cherries
Sour cream 15% fat
Sour milk
Sour milk cheese 20%
Sourdough
Spiny lobsters
Spirit
Star anise
Thyme
Umeboshi plums (Japanese apricots)
Vinegar (Apple vinegar)
Vinegar (Red wine vinegar)
Vinegar Aceto Balsamico
Walnuts roasted
White wine
Wild boar meat
Yogi tea

11 Herbs and their effects

11.1 Basil

thermal effect: warm
taste: spicy, bitter
Dries out, leads down. Tonifies Yang and Qi, dissolves mucus-cold,
eliminates wind-cold.
It has a beneficial effect on flatulence and nausea, relaxing and soothing.
Good to fight emphysema, bronchitis, whooping cough, high blood
pressure, headache, mouth odor, warts, hiccup, gout, migraine.

11.2 Mugwort

thermal effect: warm
taste: bitter, spicy
Regulates and nourishes bleeding, warms the inside, eliminates wind-
cold, eliminates parasites, eliminates heat, wetness, regulates and moves
Qi.
Reduces bleeding, alleviates pain. In the kitchen, mugwort is used as a
spice for fat food. Since it contains many bitter substances, it boosts fat
burning and promotes digestion.

11.3 Savory

thermal effect: warm
taste: bitter
Tonifies kidney yang, heart qi, stomach and spleen qi and warms the
middle, moves the liver qi and blood, releases mucous and cold from the
lungs, opens the surface, induces wind-cold.
Stomach-strengthening, soothing and appetizing. Ideal for prevent colds,
strengthens the immune system. In case of incontinence or nocturnal
wetting (not for children), put the beans in liquor for libido.

11.4 Dill

thermal effect: warm
taste: spicy
Moves qi, triggers stagnation, heads up.
The medicinal and spice herb has an antispasmodic effect and stimulates
gastric juice production. Good to fight flatulence. Antispasmodic for
gastrointestinal discomfort.

11.5 Coriander

thermal effect: warm
taste: spicy
Driving sweat, reducing wind, draining moisture, tonifying and regulating qi, eliminating wind-cold.
The essential oils are appetizing, digestive, cramping and soothing in stomach and intestinal disorders.

11.6 Herbs various

Stimulates appetite. Effect different.
Appetizing, lots of trace elements and vitamins.

11.7 Cress

thermal effect: cool
taste: sweet
Moves and tonifies qi and blood, diuretic, cools in internal heat, moisturizes lungs, triggers stagnation, heads upwards.
Diuretic, supports urination. Good to fight dry mouth, inner agitation, sore throat, diabetes, kidney stones, gastrointestinal complaints, lung problems, menstrual cramps or cancer.

11.8 Chives

thermal effect: warm
taste: spicy
Directs upward. Tonifies blood, kidney Yang and Qi. Dissolves moisture. Bactericide, prevents cancer, strengthens gastric juice production, promotes digestion and blood circulation, promotes growth, triggers stagnation.

11.9 Lovage

thermal effect: warm
taste: spicy, bitter
Reduces inner wind and moisture, dissolves stagnation, directs upward, warms Yang, regulates and moves Qi, warms inside, dissolves mucus-cold, eliminates wind-cold.
Stimulates digestion, reduces pain. Extracts of the root are used to flush out urinary tract infections and prevent kidney gravel.

11.10   Lily bulbs

thermal effect: cool
taste: sweet, bitter
Tonifies Yin, soothes Shen / Spirit. Moisturizes the lungs, clears heat and stops coughing.
Calms nerves, good to fight scaly skin. The onions and the petals are added to ointments in the Orient, which can heal muscles and tendons.
White lily (astringent).

11.11   Balm

thermal effect: warm
taste: bitter
Keep the fluids, pulls together, soothe lever fire, soothe Shen, stimulate Lung Qi. Regulates qi, eliminates heat caused by yin deficiency.
Soothing effect, Good for insomnia, restlessness and upset stomach, Allergies, Asthma, Migraine, Flatulence, Headache, Rheumatism and mental tension. To strengthen after cold and infectious diseases.

11.12   Oregano fresh

thermal effect: warm
taste: bitter
Dries out, directs down, regulates and moves Qi, eliminates wind-cold, soothes Shen / Spirit, suppresses inner wind, warms inside, eliminates wind-cold / heat-wetness, moves blood, dissolves slime-cold.
It has an anti-digestive, calming and nerve-strengthening effect, helps to fight cramping stomach and intestinal disorders. The ingredient Carvacrol has an anti-inflammatory effect.

11.13   Parsley

thermal effect: warm
taste: bitter
Nourishes blood and liver, harmonizes liver and spleen, strengthens eyesight, preserves juices, contracts. Dissolves moisture and warms Yang.
Stimulates liver function, detoxifies. Forces urinating. Relieves flatulence. Digestive and menstrual stimulating, birth-
accelerating, memory-enhancing, blood-purifying, skin-smoothing.

11.14   Peppermint

thermal effect: cool
taste: spicy, bitter
Cools heat, expels mucus, dissipates wind-cold and wind-heat, moves stomach qi, releases congestion, tonifies, regulates and moves qi.
Relaxes, frees the lungs and the nose (inhale), regulates the cycle.
Stimulates bile flow and bile production, antispasmodic in gastrointestinal disorders, antimicrobial and antiviral.

11.15   Rosemary

thermal effect: warm
taste: bitter
Dries out, leads down. Strengthens the heart, lungs and spleen qi, strengthens liver blood. Strengthens heart-Yin. Expels spleen heat / cold moisture. Strengthens spleen and kidney yang.
Promotes digestion, relieves bloating, strengthens lung, spleen and kidney. Affects the circulation and nerves. Appetizing. Baths help to fight circulatory disorders as well as with gout and rheumatism.

11.16   Sage

thermal effect: neutral
taste: bitter, spicy
Expels slime, guides down, strengthens Qi, eliminates Wind-Heat, eliminate heat induced by Yin deficiency.
Good to fight yeast infections. The leaves have a digestive effect and are used in greasy foods. Antiperspirant effect. Helps to relieve coughing attacks. Dries out (TCM).

11.17   Black caraway

thermal effect: warm
taste: spicy, sweet
Dissolve / transform moisture, tonifies Yang and Qi, moves blood, suppresses inner wind.
Detoxifying, immunoregulatory. In addition, the oil should stimulate the formation of bone marrow cells and generally protect body cells from viruses.

11.18 King Solomon's-seal

thermal effect: neutral
taste: sweet, bitter
Tonifies Yin and Qi, astringent, tonifies blood, eliminates wind-cold / heat-wetness.
Used to repair wounds or damaged tissue. Good to fight dry cough, earlier also tuberculosis and dysentery, as well as diarrhea and hemorrhoids.

11.19 Yam root, yam root tuber

thermal effect: neutral
taste: sweet
Tonifies Yin, Yang and Qi, reduces inner wind, dissolves wetness, warms Yang.
Solves cramps (in the gastrointestinal tract). Digestive through increased bile production. Anti-inflammatory in rheumatic diseases.
Mucolytic agent for coughing. Relief of menopausal symptoms.

11.20 Lemongrass

thermal effect: taste:
Diverting, calming.
Reduction of flatulence, antimicrobial, appetizing. Prevention of influenza.
Good to fight infections in the mouth and throat.

11.21 Lemon Balm (fresh)

thermal effect: cool
taste: sour
Soothes Shen / Spirit, regulates and moves Qi, eliminates heat caused by Yin deficiency, tones Qi.
Stimulating, antibacterial, encouraging, relaxing, antispasmodic, cooling, antipyretic, analgesic, sweat-inducing, virus-inhibiting. Good for colds, fever, flu, cough, bronchitis, asthma, loss of appetite, bloating, heartburn.

12 Basics of Nutrition

The basic principles of nutrition described herein are general recommendations. They are not aimed at a specific form of therapy. Recommendations concerning a therapy have priority.

12.1 Nutrition

Regular meals in a relaxed atmosphere. A warm breakfast is considered a good start into the day.
The main meals ought to be taken for lunch – supper in the early evening. Pay attention to feeling hungry or sated: don't eat too much nor remain hungry is the rule
Prepare the meals freshly from natural, regional products. Frozen, heat-conserved, industrially prepared or foodstuffs cooked in the microwave oven are rejected.
Choice of foodstuffs according to the season: more cooling food in summer, more warming food in winter.
Eat cooked food at least twice a day. Food and drinks ought to be lukewarm, never ice-cold or hot.
Raw vegetables, briefly cooked vegetables, freshly squeezed juices and mineral water are not recommended. Milk and dairy products are only included in the diet if they don't cause problems. Don't use therapeutic recipes over a longer period without consulting your doctor or therapist.

Varied food
Enjoy the diversity of foodstuffs. Characteristics of a balanced nutrition are variety, suitable combination and a balanced quantity of rich and low energy foodstuffs (on one hand avoiding undersupply with essential nutrients and on the other hand to take to many undesirable substances).

A lot of Cereal Products - and Potatoes
Bread, pasta, rice, cereal flakes (best wholemeal) as well as potatoes contain almost no fat, but many vitamins, mineral nutrients, trace elements, roughage and secondary plant substances. These foodstuffs ought to be taken with low-fat side dishes.

Vegetables and Fruit – „Take Five" every day ... 5 portions of vegetables and fruit a day, as fresh as possible, briefly cooked, or maybe one portion as a juice – ideal as a side dish to every meal as well as snack between meals: Thus a lot of vitamins, mineral nutrients as well as roughage and secondary plant substances

Daily milk and dairy products
Milk and Dairy Products every Day, once or twice per Week Fish; meat, sausages as well as eggs moderately. These foodstuffs contain valuable nutrients like calcium in the milk, iodine selenium and omega-3 fat acids in saltwater fish. Meat is favorable due to its high content of disposable iron and the vitamins B1, B6 and B12. Quantities of 300 – 600 g meat and sausage per week are sufficient. Prefer low-fat products, especially in meat- and dairy products.

Low-fat and fatty Foodstuffs
Fat supplies us with essential fat acids and fatty foodstuffs contain also fat-soluble vitamins. Fat is high in energy; therefore much fat in the food may cause overweight, possibly also cancer. Too many saturated fat acids may further a tendency for cardio-vascular diseases in the long term. Prefer vegetable oils and fats (e.g. rapeseed-, olive-, soya-oils and solid fats produced therefrom). Beware of invisible fat in meat- and dairy products, pastry and sweets as well as in fast-food and convenience foods. 70 – 90 g fat per day is sufficient.

Moderately Sugar and Salt
Take sugar and foods/drinks containing various kinds of sugar (e.g. glucose syrup) only occasionally. Use herbs and spices as well as a little salt creatively. Prefer salt containing iodine.

Plenty of Liquids
Water is absolutely essential. Drink 1-2 l liquids every day. Prefer water (with or without gas) and other low-calorie drinks. Alcoholic drinks should not be taken.

Tasty Dishes, carefully cooked
Cook the meals with as low temperatures and as short as possible, using little water and fat – this preserves the original taste, keeps the nutrients intact and prevents the production of harmful compounds.

Take time and enjoy the food
Take your Time and enjoy your Food
Eating consciously helps to eat right. The eye enjoys food, too. It's fun, invites to enjoy varied dishes and stimulates the feeling of satiety.

Watch your Weight and stay in Motion
A balanced diet and a lot of exercise and sport (30 – 60 min/day) are a healthy combination. The right weight furthers well-being and health. Thermals, directional effectiveness, digestive power

There are various criteria for judging the effectiveness of herbs and foodstuffs.

The use of certain herbs and ingredients is based on observations of the effects on the body which these foodstuffs, herbs and spices show after having eaten them. The medical science has developed following system: Every ingredient or herb has a directional effectiveness. Furthermore, there are herbs which have a special effect on certain organs.

The basic condition for a healthy metabolism is to obtain sufficient energy from food and that the digestive process doesn't use too much energy. An easily digestible meal makes content and sated, doesn't cause flatulence and fatigue after the meal. The perfect spices increase the healthiness of our meals. Very often, just small doses of herbs and spices will suffice. They are not used to make us sated, but to help our digestive organs to digest the food.

12.2 Recipes

The recipes list the ingredients to be used and the cooking instructions show how the dish is prepared. The list of ingredients shows the concerned quantities as well as the relevance for the therapy. If you find „less than mentioned", try to comply or find an alternative from the „list of recommended foodstuffs". Mostly it shall result just in a small change of taste when you simply avoid this ingredient.

Mild cooking methods: boiling, stewing, poaching, steaming
Strong cooking methods: barbecuing, roasting, frying, smoking
Balanced cooking methods: deep-frying, baking brick
Deep-freezing and warming in the microwave oven should be avoided (denaturalization).

12.3 Foodstuffs

Foodstuffs have an effect on body and soul like medicinal herbs, only a very much milder one. Dietary advice is mainly based on regional foodstuffs. The knowledge about the effects of each foodstuff and the knowledge, when which foodstuff shall be used, is based on the orthodox school of medicine. Use ecologic-organic products, if possible. As everything should be cooked for a long time due to a better digestability and very rarely eaten raw, the food agrees with everyone.

The classification of the foodstuffs according to their effect on the body is the basis in order to achieve a harmonious status of health.

Dietary advisors do not recommend certain foodstuffs for everyone. The individual diet is tailor-made for the individual constitution.

Buy only fresh and ripe fruit and vegetables. You ought to leave unripe fruit and vegetables and such with brown spots and wilted leaves behind in the market. In this case take deep-frozen goods (never ready-to-serve dishes!). Fruit and vegetables are deep-frozen immediately after harvesting and often contain more vitamins and minerals than the goods from the vegetable shelf. Whereas conserved or tinned goods contain very much less biological substances. Also, salt, sugar and others are mostly added to the latter. Never leave the foodstuffs in the water after washing them to avoid that many vital substances get drowned. Clean salads, fruit and vegetables immediately before serving.

Please make sure of the hygienic processing of foodstuffs. Clean your salads, fruit and vegetables carefully. When cooking with meat, prepare all ingredients first and then process the meat products. Clean the worktop and tools very carefully. Wooden surfaces ought to be treated with a mild disinfectant regularly in order to reduce germination.
Store fruit and vegetables separately, if possible. Harvested fruit and vegetables are still alive and emit e.g. ethylene gas, which makes other products ripen and age faster. Keep meat and fish in the closed packaging or store them in the fridge in closed containers.

12.4 Herbs

There are some basic rules for storing medicinal herbs. On principle, herbs must be protected from direct sunlight, humidity and heat.

Containers for the storage of herbs may be glasses, ceramic jars and even plastic containers. However, plastic is a rather unsuitable material and should only be a short-term solution. In case of glass containers, use a dark material.

Medicinal herbs cannot be kept for any long period. The shelf life of herbs is limited. However, it can be prolonged with suitable storage. The place should be dark, rather cool and absolutely dry. A wooden medicine cabinet, placed not directly next to a source of heat, would be ideal. Never buy large quantities of herbs so as not to have to throw them away. Label the container with the name of the herb and the date of harvesting or processing.

13 Other dietic-books

The following syndromes of dietetics, TCM or for a therapy supplement for cancer are available.

Dietetics

E001. Nutrition of the infant - baby food
E002. Nutrition during lactation
E003. Nutrition in old age
E004. Nutrition of children and adolescents
E005. Nutrition of athletes
E006. Light weight
E007. Pregnancy
E008. Full food

Protein and electrolyte - kidneys

E009. (hemodialysis) dialysis treatment
E010. Acute renal failure
E011. Chronic renal insufficiency
E012. Nephrotic syndrome
E013. Kidney stones (nephrolithiasis)

Gastrointestinal tract - pancreas

E014. Acute pancreatitis (inflammation of the pancreas)
E015. Chronic pancreatitis (inflammation of the pancreas)

Gastrointestinal tract - small intestine and large intestine

E016. Acute obstipation (constipation)
E017. Chronic obstipation (constipation)
E018. Colon irritabile
E019. Diverticulitis
E020. Acquired lactose intolerance (lactose malabsorption)
E021. Fructose malabsorption
E022. Glutensensitive enteropathy (celiac disease)
E023. Colectomy
E024. Short Bowel Syndrome

Gastrointestinal tract - liver, gallbladder, bile ducts

E025. Acute and chronic hepatitis (inflammation of the liver)
E026. Cholelithiasis (bile stones)
E027. fatty liver
E028. cirrhosis

Gastrointestinal tract - Stomach and duodenal intestine

E029. Acute gastritis
E030. Chronic gastritis
E031. Stomach bleeding
E032. Ulcus ventriculi and duodenal ulcer
E033. Condition after gastric surgery

Gastrointestinal tract - oral cavity and esophagus
E034. Stomatitis
E035. Esophageal carcinoma (esophageal cancer)
E036. Refluosophagitis (heartburn)

Special diseases
E037. Phenylketonuria (PKU)
E038. Rheumatic joint diseases

Metabolism
E039. Obesity (overweight)
E040. Diabetes mellitus
E041. Eating disorders (underweight)

Fat metabolism
E042. Hypercholesterolaemia (increased cholesterol level)
E043. Hepatic Encephalopathy

Heart and circulation
E044. Arteriosclerosis (arterial calcification)
E045. Heart insufficiency
E046. Hypertension
E047. Hyperuricaemia and gout

Changed nutrient requirements
E048. In case of fever
E049. For malignant diseases
E050. After burns
E051. Radiation and chemotherapy

CANCER
E100. Pancreatic cancer
E101. Bladder cancer
E102. Blood cancer (leukemia)
E103. Breast cancer
E104. Colorectal cancer
E105. Gastric cancer
E106. Kidney cancer
E107. Esophageal cancer

TCM
E200. Bladder - moisture heat in the bladder
E201. Bladder - moisture and cold in the bladder
E202. Bladder - emptiness and cold in the bladder
E203. Large intestine - external cold affects the large intestine
E204. Large intestine - moisture heat in the large intestine
E205. Large intestine - heat blocks the intestine II acute
E206. Large intestine - dryness of the colon
E207. Large intestine - Yang deficiency (cold)
E208. Heart - Blood insufficiency
E209. Heart - Blood stagnation
E210. Heart - Fire
E211. Heart - Hot mucus clogs the heart pores

E212. Heart - Cold mucus clogs the heart pores
E213. Heart - Qi deficiency
E214. Heart - Yang deficiency
E215. Heart - Yin deficiency
E216. Liver - Ascending Liver Yang
E217. Liver - Blood deficiency
E218. Liver - Blood stagnation
E219. Liver - Moisture heat in liver and gall bladder
E220. Liver - Fire
E221. Liver - Gall bladder Qi-Empty
E222. Liver - Cold in the liver meridian
E223. Liver - Qi stagnation
E224. Liver - Wind
E225. Liver - Wind with ascending liver Yang
E226. Liver - Wind with blood anemic
E227. Liver - Wind with extreme heat
E228. Lung - Qi deficiency
E229. Lung - Mucus-moisture in the lungs
E230. Lung - Mucus-heat in the lungs
E231. Lung - Mucus-cold in the lungs
E232. Lung - Dryness of the lungs
E233. Lung - Wind-heat attacks the lungs
E234. Lung - Wind-cold affects the lungs
E235. Lung - Yin deficiency
E236. Stomach - Bloodstagnation
E237. Stomach - Fire
E238. Stomach - Cold with liquid
E239. Stomach - Nutrition stagnation
E240. Stomach - Qi deficiency
E241. Stomach - Rebellious Qi
E242. Stomach - Yin Emptiness
E243. Spleen - Heat and moisture attack the spleen
E244. Spleen - Coldness and moisture affects the spleen
E245. Spleen - Qi deficiency
E246. Spleen - Qi deficiency + Declining spleen Qi
E247. Spleen - Qi deficiency + spleen does not control the blood
E248. Spleen - Yang deficiency
E249. Kidney - Heart and kidney no longer communicate
E250. Kidney - Jing deficiency
E251. Kidney - Kidneys cannot receive the Qi
E252. Kidney - Qi is not stable
E253. Kidney - Yang deficiency
E254. Kidney - Yin deficiency

For further information visit di-book.com.